COSMOPRESS

COVER: "COUNT ALPHONSE DE TOULOUSE-LAUTREC, THE ARTIST'S FATHER" WAS PAINTED BY HENRI WHEN HE WAS ONLY 17 YEARS OLD. THE SON AND THE GRANDSON OF EXPERT HORSEMEN, THIS ARTIST DEMONSTRATED AT AN EARLY AGE A PROFOUND UNDERSTANDING FOR THE CHARACTER, BEAUTY AND SPIRIT OF THE HORSE.

HENRI'S BEARDED FATHER SITS AT EASE IN THE SADDLE. HE AND THE HORSE ARE ONE. HIS ATTENTION IS DIRECTED TO THE HOVERING FALCON.

THE MORNING SUN TINTS THE LOW-LYING CLOUDS WITH TONES OF GOLD AND RED. IT IS A BEAUTIFUL DAY FOR MAN, BIRD AND ANIMAL.

PERFORMING HORSE AND MONKEY   MUSEUM OF ALBI

DEDICATED TO JENNIE AND WILLIAM RABOFF, MY PARENTS

WORLD RIGHTS RESERVED BY ERNEST RABOFF AND GEMINI-SMITH, INC. ISBN Trade: 0-385-04942-0
LIBRARY OF CONGRESS CATALOGUE CARD NO. 78-93207   Library: 0-385-07206-6
PRINTED IN JAPAN BY TOPPAN

HENRI DE TOULOUSE-LAUTREC

By *Ernest Raboff*

ART FOR CHILDREN

A GEMINI-SMITH BOOK

EDITED BY BRADLEY SMITH

PUBLISHED BY

DOUBLEDAY & CO., INC.

GARDEN CITY, NEW YORK

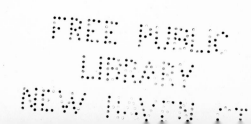

HENRI DE TOULOUSE-LAUTREC (TO-LOOZ' LO-TREK') WAS
BORN ON NOVEMBER 24, 1864, IN THE TOWN OF ALBI IN
SOUTHERN FRANCE. HE DIED IN ALBI WHEN ONLY 37 YEARS OLD.

HIS FATHER, ALPHONSE, WAS A RICH NOBLEMAN. HIS MOTHER,
ADÈLE, WAS A BEAUTIFUL AND INTELLIGENT WOMAN WHO
ENCOURAGED HENRI DURING HIS ACTIVE BUT DIFFICULT LIFE.
UNLIKE MANY ARTISTS, TOULOUSE-LAUTREC NEVER WORRIED
ABOUT MONEY AND WAS UNCONCERNED WITH SUCCESS.

AS A BOY, HENRI SUFFERED TWO ACCIDENTS WHICH KEPT HIS
ALREADY WEAK LEGS FROM GROWING. HE MOVED WITH THE
AID OF A WALKING STICK AND ONLY REACHED A HEIGHT OF
LESS THAN 5 FEET. YET HIS CHEST AND ARMS WERE POWERFUL.
FROM THE AGE OF 8 AND FOR THE
REST OF HIS LIFE TOULOUSE-LAUTREC
PAINTED SHOPGIRLS, COUNTESSES,
WASHERWOMEN, ACTORS, CLOWNS,
ACROBATS, DOGS — AND A
FAVORITE SUBJECT, HORSES.

PORTRAIT OF LAUTREC
BY ERNEST RABOFF

HIS FREELY REALISTIC STYLE, FULL
OF LIFE, WIT AND MOTION, AND HIS
MASTERY OF PEN AND BRUSH BROUGHT
HIM FAME IN HIS LIFETIME AND EARNED
FOR HIM A PERMANENT PLACE IN
THE GALLERIES OF THE WORLD.

HENRI DE TOULOUSE-LAUTREC'S GRANDMOTHER FONDLY RECALLED THAT HE SANG FROM MORNING TO NIGHT AS A CHILD. "HE IS A REAL CRICKET AND ENLIVENS THE WHOLE HOUSE-HOLD. HIS PRESENCE FILLS THE HOUSE LIKE THAT OF 20 PEOPLE."

WHEN THE ARTIST WAS 4 YEARS OLD HE ASKED TO ADD HIS SIGNATURE IN THE GUEST BOOK AT THE CHRISTENING OF HIS BROTHER. "BUT YOU CAN'T WRITE," SAID HIS MOTHER. "IT DOESN'T MATTER, I'LL DRAW AN OX", REPLIED HENRI.

A FRIEND, HENRI RACHOU, WROTE: "HIS MOST STRIKING CHARAC-TERISTICS... WERE HIS OUTSTANDING INTELLIGENCE AND CONSTANT ALERTNESS, HIS ABUNDANT GOOD WILL... AND HIS PROFOUND UNDERSTANDING OF HIS FELLOW MEN."

E. SCHAUB-KOCH WROTE: "LAUTREC'S NAME STANDS FOR.. A VISION OF THINGS ...KEENNESS OF MIND...SENSIBILITY. IT STANDS FOR A STATE OF SOUL..." LAUTREC HAD A SUPERB TECHNIQUE AND A DEEP SPIRITUAL QUALITY.

TOULOUSE-LAUTREC OFTEN SAID: "LIFE IS BEAUTIFUL! HOW BEAUTIFUL LIFE IS!"

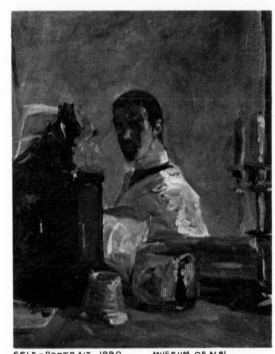

SELF-PORTRAIT, 1880   MUSEUM OF ALBI

"THE COMTESSE ADÈLE DE TOULOUSE-LAUTREC IN THE DINING ROOM" IS A PAINTING THAT SHOWS US THE STRENGTH, DIGNITY AND BEAUTY THIS GENTLE WOMAN BROUGHT INTO THE LIFE OF HER ARTIST-SON.

FROM HIS EARLIEST CHILDHOOD DAYS HIS MOTHER BELIEVED IN HER SON'S ABUNDANT INTELLIGENCE AND KNEW FROM HIS FIRST DRAWINGS THAT HENRI WAS GIFTED WITH GREAT TALENT.

THIS PAINTING OF THE COMTESSE REFLECT'S HENRI'S KNOWLEDGE OF THE IMPORTANCE HIS MOTHER PLAYED IN DEVELOPING AND PROTECTING HIS PRECIOUS ARTISTIC GIFTS.

HER YOUTHFUL FACE IS LIKE A SUN FULL OF WARMTH AND QUIETNESS, MODESTY AND COMPASSION. SHE SITS ON HER DINING CHAIR LIKE A WISE AND GENTLE QUEEN.

THE SOFT MORNING LIGHT COMING THROUGH THE WINDOW ADDS TO THE FEELING OF PEACE AND TRAN-QUILITY THE ARTIST HAS CAPTURED ON HIS CANVAS.

COMTESSE ADÈLE DE TOULOUSE-LAUTREC IN THE DINING ROOM, 1887   MUSEUM OF ALBI

"COUNT DE TOULOUSE-LAUTREC DRIVING THE MAIL COACH TO NICE" SHOWS LAUTREC'S GREAT LOVE OF ACTION.

THE TEAM OF FOUR HORSES RACING DOWN THE ROADWAY, THEIR FLYING HOOVES RAISING CLOUDS OF DUST, IS PULLING THE COACH SO EVENLY THAT THE GENTLEMAN SEATED IN THE CARRIAGE IS RESTING SECURELY WITH ARMS FOLDED ACROSS HIS CHEST. HE IS LIKE A MAN LEANING AGAINST THE SIDE OF A BUILDING IDLY WATCHING THE TRAFFIC GO BY.

IT IS LAUTREC'S FATHER, ALPHONSE, WHO IS DRIVING THE TEAM. KNOWING HIS FATHER'S ADMIRATION FOR THESE MAGNIFICENT ANIMALS, YOUNG HENRI STARTED AT AN EARLY AGE TO RECORD SCENES LIKE THIS ONE TO PLEASE HIM. IN SO DOING, HE DREW AND PAINTED SOME OF THE FINEST IMPRESSIONS OF HORSES IN ACTION IN ALL THE HISTORY OF ART.

COUNT DE TOULOUSE-LAUTREC DRIVING THE MAIL COACH TO NICE, 1881   MUSÉE DU PETIT PALAIS, PARIS

"SOUVENIR D'AUTEUIL" IS A FASCINATING EXAMPLE OF TOULOUSE-LAUTREC'S EARLY MASTERY OF PAINTING. IT WAS DONE BY HIM IN HIS SEVENTEENTH YEAR.

HIS EYES COULD RECORD AND HIS HAND COULD TRANSLATE INTO PAINTED STROKES THE BRANCHES AND LEAVES, TREE TRUNKS AND MEADOWS, HUMAN FIGURES AND ANIMALS, BUCKETS AND CLOTHING, GESTURES AND ACTION WITH ASTOUNDING ACCURACY.

THE GROOM BRUSHING THE HORSE, THE MAN HOLDING THE BRIDLE, THE SHORT LAUTREC AND HIS TALL ART TEACHER, PRINCETEAU — SEEN BEYOND THE HORSE'S BACK — THE TWO SILK-HATTED SPORTS-MEN CREATE A MAGIC CIRCLE FOR ONE TO STUDY AND EXPLORE.

THE COLORFUL CLOTHING ON THE GRASS, THE GRAZING HORSE, THE TREES AT THE REAR OF THE FIELD AND THE LADIES WAITING IN THE SHADE FORM AN OUTER CIRCLE THAT COMPLETES THE STORY OF THIS CHARMING SCENE.

SOUVENIR D'AUTEUIL   GIRAUDON FROM RAPHO GUILLUMETTE

"GABRIEL TAPIE DE CELEYRAN" WAS TOULOUSE-LAUTREC'S FAVORITE COUSIN AND LIFELONG FRIEND. THIS PORTRAIT IS A MASTERPIECE OF FIGURE PAINTING.

THE TILT OF THE HEAD, THE SLOPE OF THE SHOULDERS, THE RESTFUL STANCE, ALL ADD TO THE THOUGHTFUL EXPRESSION ON THE FACE OF THIS MAN.

A THEATER'S BACKSTAGE IS USED AS A SETTING BY LAUTREC TO ADD SIGNIFICANCE AND TO BROADEN OUR UNDER-STANDING OF GABRIEL DE CELEYRAN. THIS SCHOLAR WAS A MAN OF THE WORLD. HE WAS EQUALLY AT HOME IN THE BRIGHT LIGHTS AND GAY GATHERINGS IN THE THEATER AND IN THE SERIOUS CLASSROOMS OF THE UNIVERSITY.

DR. GABRIEL TAPIE DE CELEYRAN DEVOTED THE LAST 30 YEARS OF HIS LIFE TO PROMOTING THE GENIUS OF HIS FRIEND AND COUSIN. HE WAS ONE OF THE FOUNDERS OF THE ALBI MUSEUM, WHICH IS DEDICATED TO THE WORK OF ALBI'S MOST FAMOUS CITIZEN, HENRI DE TOULOUSE-LAUTREC.

GABRIEL TAPIE DE CELEYRAN   MUSEUM OF ALBI

"PORTRAIT OF VINCENT VAN GOGH" PORTRAYS ANOTHER GOOD FRIEND OF TOULOUSE-LAUTREC. THEY BOTH EXHIBITED THEIR PAINTINGS AT THE GALLERY OF VAN GOGH'S BROTHER, THEO.

IT WAS HENRI WHO SUGGESTED THAT VAN GOGH TRAVEL TO THE SOUTH OF FRANCE TO PAINT THE COUNTRYSIDE OF SUN AND COLOR.

THE DUTCH ARTIST LISTENED TO HIS FRIEND'S ADVICE AND WENT TO ARLES, WHERE HE CREATED MANY MASTERPIECES WITH HIS SUNLIT STROKES OF COLOR.

LAUTREC DREW THIS POWERFUL PORTRAIT IN PASTEL CHALKS.

COUNT CHAS. DE TOULOUSE-LAUTREC, THE ARTIST'S UNCLE, 1882   MUSEUM OF ALBI

PORTRAIT OF VINCENT VAN GOGH STEDELIJK MUSEUM

"JANE AVRIL AT THE JARDIN DE PARIS" IS ONE
OF LAUTREC'S MANY MAGNIFICENT LITHOGRAPHS.

HENRI DE TOULOUSE-LAUTREC'S CONTRIBUTION TO
LITHOGRAPHY WAS TO DRAW WITH COLORED CRAYONS
ON LIMESTONE WHICH WAS THEN PRINTED ON PAPER
BY A HAND PRESS. HIS SWEEPING LINES AND BOLD
COLORS ENRICHED AND DEVELOPED THIS ART FORM.

HE LEARNED MUCH ABOUT *THE* USE OF SHARP OUTLINES AND
PURE FLAT COLORS FROM HIS STUDIES OF WOOD-BLOCK
PRINTS BY SUCH JAPANESE MASTERS AS HOKUSAI AND HIROSHIGE.

JANE AVRIL, THE DANCER SHOWN IN THIS POSTER, WROTE
IN HER MEMOIRS: "IT IS TO LAUTREC I OWE MY FAME,
WHICH DATES FROM THE APPEARANCE OF HIS FIRST
POSTER OF ME."

JANE AVRIL AT THE JARDIN DE PARIS, 1893   MUSEUM OF ALBI

"THE DANCE AT THE MOULIN-ROUGE" FOCUSES OUR
ATTENTION AT THE CENTER OF THE FLOOR.

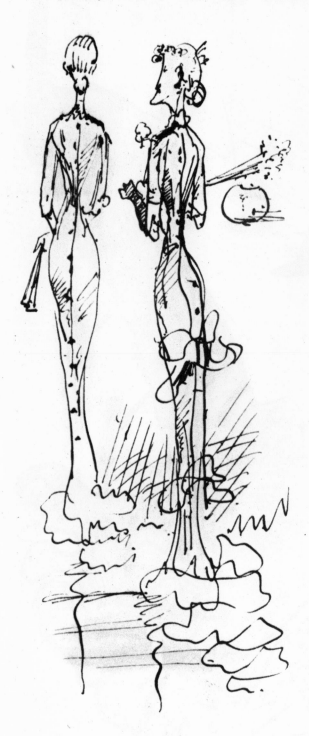

THE FIRST THING WE
NOTICE IS THE COUPLE
DANCING.

THE WOMAN'S FLOATING
HAIR, THE CURVE OF HER
ARM HOLDING UP HER SKIRT,
THE RED STOCKINGS, THE
HIGH-KICKING LEG AND HER
SUPPORTING LEG ON TIP TOE
ARE REPEATED IN THE SOFT
BLUE SHADOW ON THE FLOOR.

VALENTIN LE DESOSSÉ, A
WELL-KNOWN VISITOR TO
THE PARIS NIGHTCLUBS, IS
HER GRACEFUL PARTNER.

ONLY A FEW PEOPLE SEEM
TO BE WATCHING THEIR
PERFORMANCE.

BUT THE DANCE IS THE ONLY THING OF IMPORTANCE
FOR THE DANCERS AND FOR THE ARTIST, LAUTREC.

THE DANCE AT THE MOULIN-ROUGE, 1890   HENRY P. MC ILHENNY COL., PHILADELPHIA

AT THE MOULIN-ROUGE, A PARIS NIGHTCLUB, LAUTREC
FOUND THE MOST INTERESTING AND INSPIRING SUBJECTS
AND CHARACTERS FOR HIS PAINTBRUSH.

HE LOVED THE THEATER, THE DANCE,
THE SPECTATORS
AND ABOVE ALL,
THE ARTISTS WHO PER-
FORMED. BEING AN ARTIST
HIMSELF, HE UNDERSTOOD
HOW MUCH THEY GAVE
IN CREATING THEIR ART.

THE LADIES AND GENTLE-
MEN SEATED AROUND
THE TABLES MIGHT BE
FOUND TODAY—EXCEPT
FOR THEIR CLOTHING
STYLES—WITH THE SAME
EXPRESSIONS ON THEIR
FACES, IN ANY NIGHTCLUB ANYWHERE.

TOULOUSE-LAUTREC, WHO SPENT SO MUCH OF HIS TIME
IN PLACES LIKE THE MOULIN-ROUGE, HAS PAINTED HIMSELF
AND HIS COUSIN, GABRIEL DE CELEYRAN, IN THE CENTER
BACKGROUND WALKING PAST A TABLE.

AT THE MOULIN-ROUGE, 1892   THE ART INSTITUTE OF CHICAGO, HELEN BIRCH BARTLETT MEMORIAL COL.

"JANE AVRIL LEAVING THE MOULIN-ROUGE,"
AFTER HER EVENING'S WORK OF DANCING, GLOWS
WITH THE RESPECT AND ADMIRATION LAUTREC HELD FOR
THIS ATTRACTIVE AND TALENTED FELLOW ARTIST.

HER FACE IS A
BEAUTIFUL STUDY OF
QUIET THOUGHTS, MAKING
THE WALK HOME A PLEASANT
AND REFLECTIVE ONE.

HANDS TUCKED IN HER
POCKETS FOR WARMTH,
HER BLUE FLOWERED
BONNET, BLUE COAT,
SKIRT AND SHOES ALL
SUGGEST THE CONTENTED
WEARINESS THAT FILLS
THE DANCER AFTER A WELL-
DONE PERFORMANCE.

THE ARTIST MAKES THE MOOD OF THIS PAINTING
A WARMLY PLEASING ONE BY SURROUNDING
THE DANCER WITH FLECKS OF GOLDEN LIGHT
FROM THE PARIS STREET LAMPS.

JANE AVRIL LEAVING THE MOULIN-ROUGE, 1892   WADSWORTH ATHENEUM, HARTFORD, CONNECTICUT

"IN THE CIRCUS FERNANDO : *THE RINGMASTER*" IS ANOTHER
EXCITING PAINTING BY LAUTREC OF A HORSE IN ACTION.
HIS LOVE FOR THE CIRCUS BEGAN IN HIS CHILDHOOD
WHEN HIS FATHER AND HIS ART TEACHER, PRINCETEAU,
TOOK HIM "TO SEE THE HORSES".

THE CIRCUS ADDED MORE CHALLENGES TO HIS GROWING
TALENT. THERE WERE *THE RINGMASTER* WITH HIS LONG
WHIP, THE FROLICKING CLOWN, THE BENCHES CIRCLING
THE ARENA, AND THE SPECTATORS.

THE WOMAN RIDER'S GAZE IS FASTENED ON THE
RINGMASTER'S FACE. FOLLOWING THE ARCHED NECK
OF THE HORSE, THE CURVING WHIP, THE FLOWING
HORSE'S TAIL, OUR OWN ATTENTION MOVES AROUND
THE PAINTING IN A WIDENING ARC AS WE STUDY
EVERY DETAIL.

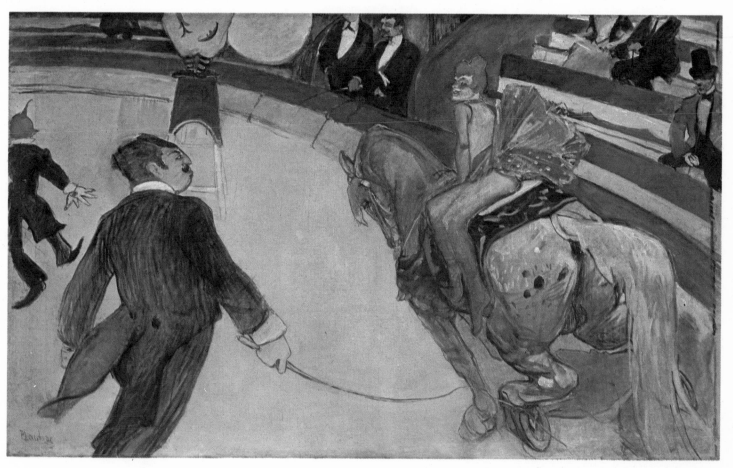

IN THE CIRCUS FERNANDO : THE RINGMASTER , 1888 THE ART INSTITUTE OF CHICAGO, MR. AND MRS. L. COBURN MEMORIAL COL.

CIPA GODEBSKY WAS A GOOD FRIEND AND FELLOW
ARTIST OF TOULOUSE-LAUTREC.

THE TWO MEN, THE POLISH SCULPTOR AND THE
FRENCH PAINTER, HAD PLANNED TO WRITE A BOOK
TOGETHER, BUT BECAME TOO BUSY WITH THEIR
INDIVIDUAL WORK TO GET PAST THE FIRST SENTENCE.

IT COULD HAVE BEEN A VERY AMUSING BOOK.
LAUTREC WAS A GREAT WIT AND HIS PORTRAIT OF
GODEBSKY SHOWS US A MAN WITH LAUGHING EYES
ABOVE A HINT OF A SMILE AND WITH A HUMOROUS
EXPRESSION PLAYING AROUND HIS FACE.

NOTICE THE STRENGTH OF THE SCULPTOR'S HAND.
THE MUSCULAR ARM, BROAD BACK AND THICK NECK
CREATE AN IMAGE OF A POWERFUL, SENSITIVE MAN.

PORTRAIT OF CIPA GODEBSKY, 1896   STAVROS S. NIARCHOS COLLECTION

"WOMAN IN A STUDIO" IS AN EARLY LAUTREC MASTERPIECE.

HE PAINTED THIS WORK SHORTLY AFTER HE FINISHED
HIS STUDIES WITH FERNAND CORMON, HIS TEACHER.

THE LAUNDRESS

CARMEN GAUDIER, THE
MODEL HERE, WAS A
WORKING GIRL WHO ADDED
TO HER INCOME BY
POSING FOR ARTISTS.

SHE HAD A LOVELY
THOUGHTFUL FACE. HER
ARMS AND HANDS, LIKE THOSE
OF THE PAINTERS FOR
WHOM SHE SAT,
COULD MAKE A DIS-
ORDERED ROOM INTO A
PLACE OF SPARKLING
BEAUTY OR MAKE A BAG
OF LAUNDRY INTO
SNOWY-CLEAN AND
IRONED SHEETS AND SHIRTS.

USING THE TECHNIQUE OF THE IMPRESSIONISTS, STROKES
OF SUN-BRIGHT COLOR, LAUTREC BECAME A MODERN PAINTER
AT THE VERY BEGINNING OF HIS PROFESSIONAL CAREER.

WOMAN IN A STUDIO   MUSEUM OF FINE ARTS, BOSTON   BEQUEST OF JOHN T. SPAULDING

DEC 9   1976

DEC 9   1976